WEALTH WISDOM

BEYOND THE BALANCE SHEET

-Ramesh Chauhan

Title: *Wealth Wisdom: Beyond the Balance Sheet*
Author: Ramesh Chauhan
Publisher: Independently published
ISBN: 9798344220420
Edition: First Edition
Published Date: 23 october 2024
Copyright: © [2024], Ramesh Chauhan
All rights reserved.

Dedication

To all those who are seeking more than just financial success,
To the dreamers, the disciplined, and the determined,
And to my family, whose support and love are the true riches of my life.
This book is for you.

Epigraph

"Wealth consists not in having great possessions, but in having few wants."
—Epictetus

Preface

In a world where financial success is often equated with happiness, I've learned that true wealth goes far beyond numbers and balance sheets. It's about the quality of life we lead, the relationships we nurture, the health we maintain, and the fulfillment we find in everyday moments. For years, I believed that accumulating more money would lead to more happiness, but I found myself at a crossroads where wealth, in its most material form, wasn't delivering on its promise. This realization led me on a journey to discover that wealth is multidimensional and deeply personal.

Wealth Wisdom: Beyond the Balance Sheet is the culmination of my reflections on what it really means to live a wealthy life. In these pages, you'll find stories, research, and practical advice that challenge conventional wisdom about wealth and encourage you to redefine what success means to you. This book is not just about managing money; it's about managing life—and finding balance, happiness, and purpose along the way.

Acknowledgments

Writing *Wealth Wisdom: Beyond the Balance Sheet* has been an enriching journey, one that I could not have completed without the support, guidance, and inspiration of many individuals. First and foremost, I am deeply grateful to my family, whose unwavering love, patience, and belief in me have been my true foundation of wealth. Your presence in my life is a constant reminder of what truly matters.

I must also express my heartfelt gratitude to the many authors, researchers, and thought leaders whose ideas, directly or indirectly, inspired this book. Your insights into psychology, personal finance, and behavioral economics provided me with a broader perspective and a deeper understanding of how wealth is far more than just numbers. Special thanks to writers like Morgan Housel, Daniel Kahneman, and Chip and Dan Heath, whose works served as intellectual stepping stones throughout this writing process.

To my readers and colleagues, thank you for the insightful conversations and reflections on wealth, success, and life. Your thoughts and shared experiences helped shape many of the ideas presented in this book. I am forever grateful for your input and encouragement.

Lastly, to every individual who has shared their personal stories of financial struggle, success, and everything in between—your experiences reminded me that the journey toward true wealth is unique for everyone, and it's as much about self-discovery as it is about financial growth.

Thank you for inspiring me to look beyond the numbers and into the heart of what it means to live a truly wealthy life.

CONTENT

Dedication — 3
Epigraph — 3
Preface — 4
Acknowledgments — 5
Introduction: Redefining Wealth — 15
    The Emotional Price of Financial Success — 15
    The Hidden Side of Wealth — 16
Part 1: The Mindset for Wealth — 19
    Chapter 1: Patience is the Ultimate Wealth Strategy — 19
        The Power of Patience and Delayed Gratification — 19
        The Marshmallow Test and Its Wealth Implications — 20
        The Power of Compound Interest — 20
        Examples of Patience in Action — 21
        Practical Takeaway: How to Cultivate Patience in Your Financial Life — 22
        Conclusion: Wealth is Built Over Time, Not Overnight — 23
    Chapter 2: Emotional Intelligence in Wealth Management — 25
        The Power of Emotional Intelligence in Financial Success — 25
        Emotional Intelligence and Decision-Making — 26

How Emotional Intelligence Affects Financial Decisions — 26

Emotions and Market Volatility — 27

Stories of Emotion-Driven Financial Choices — 28

The Panic Seller — 28

The Overconfident Investor — 28

Practical Takeaway: Strategies to Boost Your Emotional Intelligence in Financial Decisions — 29

1. Practice Self-Awareness — 29

2. Develop Mindfulness — 29

3. Set Rules for Yourself — 30

4. Seek Outside Perspectives — 30

5. Focus on the Long-Term — 30

Conclusion: Emotional Intelligence—The Hidden Superpower in Wealth Management — 31

Chapter 3: Self-Sabotage—How We Get in Our Own Way — 32

Overcoming Self-Sabotage in Wealth Management — 32

Understanding Self-Sabotage and Its Roots — 32

1. Examples of Self-Sabotage in Wealth Management — 33

2. The Psychological Roots of Self-Sabotage — 34

3. How Past Experiences Shape Our Relationship with Money — 35

Practical Takeaway: How to Overcome Self-Sabotage and Build Healthy Financial Habits — 36

1. Identify Your Self-Sabotaging Habits — 36
2. Dig Deeper into the Root Cause — 36
3. Reframe Limiting Beliefs — 37
4. Build Healthy Financial Habits — 37

Conclusion: Mastering Your Inner Game of Wealth — 38

Part 2: Building a Strong Wealth Foundation — 39

Chapter 4: Discipline—The Foundation of Wealth — 39

Discipline as the Cornerstone of Wealth-Building — 39

Understanding the Role of Discipline in Wealth — 39

1. The Importance of Financial Discipline in Budgeting, Saving, and Investing — 40
2. Stories of Individuals Who Built Wealth Slowly But Steadily Through Discipline — 40
3. The Short-Term Pleasures of Spending vs. The Long-Term Rewards of Discipline — 41

Practical Takeaway: How to Cultivate Financial Discipline — 42

1. Automate Your Savings and Investments — 42
2. Set Realistic Budgets — 43
3. Build Habits Through Routines — 43
4. Break Goals into Small, Manageable Milestones — 44
5. Focus on Your "Why" — 44

Conclusion: The Power of Discipline in Wealth-Building — 44

Chapter 5: Overcoming Instant Gratification ... 46

  Resisting Instant Gratification in a Culture of Now ... 46

  Understanding Instant Gratification and Its Impact on Wealth ... 46

    1. Why Humans Are Wired for Instant Gratification ... 46

    2. The Cost of Instant Gratification—How It Leads to Debt and Financial Trouble ... 47

    3. Case Studies of People Who Overcame Instant Gratification and Built Lasting Wealth ... 48

  Practical Takeaway: How to Shift Your Mindset from Instant Gratification to Long-Term Success ... 50

    1. Create a "Pause Button" for Purchases ... 50

    2. Visualize Your Long-Term Financial Goals ... 50

    3. Build Rewards for Delayed Gratification ... 51

    4. Focus on Experiences, Not Things ... 51

  Conclusion: Mastering the Urge for Instant Gratification ... 52

Chapter 6: The Role of Habits in Financial Success ... 53

  Wealth is a Result of Consistent Habits ... 53

  The Power of Small Habits and Financial Compounding ... 53

    1. The Power of Compounding—In Both Finance and Behavior ... 53

    2. Atomic Habits: Small Changes, Big Results ... 54

3. Real-Life Examples of Wealth-Building Habits   55

Practical Takeaway: Building Small Financial Habits for Long-Term Success   56

1. Start with One or Two Small Changes   56
2. Automate Your Habits   57
3. Track Your Progress   57
4. Build Positive Reinforcement Into Your Habits   57

Conclusion: Consistency is Key to Financial Success   58

Part 3: Beyond the Balance Sheet—True Wealth   59

Chapter 7: The Happiness Factor—Why Money Isn't Enough   59

True Wealth Goes Beyond Financial Security   59

Why More Money Doesn't Lead to More Happiness   59

1. The Hedonic Treadmill: Why We Always Want More   59
2. Stories of Wealthy Individuals Who Found Happiness Beyond Money   60
3. Research on Wealth and Happiness: Where's the Tipping Point?   61

Practical Takeaway: Cultivating Happiness Alongside Financial Success   62

1. Focus on Meaningful Work and Purpose   62
2. Invest in Relationships   63

    3. Pursue Personal Passions   63

    4. Practice Gratitude and Mindfulness   63

Conclusion: Wealth with Happiness—A Balanced Approach   64

Chapter 8: Health and Well-Being—The Greatest Wealth   65

Wealth and Well-Being Must Go Hand in Hand   65

The Link Between Health and Financial Success   66

    1. The Price of Burnout and Chronic Stress   66

    2. Stories of Wealth at the Cost of Health   66

    3. Balancing Ambition with Self-Care   67

Practical Takeaway: Integrating Health and Well-Being into Wealth-Building   68

    1. Manage Stress Proactively   68

    2. Make Physical Activity Non-Negotiable   68

    3. Prioritize Sleep   69

    4. Practice Mindful Eating   69

    5. Set Health-Related Goals Alongside Financial Goals   70

Conclusion: True Wealth is a Balance Between Health and Financial Success   70

Chapter 9: Relationships—The Currency of Connection   72

Wealth Means Little Without Strong Relationships   72

Key Topics: 73

1. The Danger of Sacrificing Relationships for Wealth and Status ... 73

2. Redefining Wealth by Nurturing Personal Connections ... 74

3. Research on the Power of Relationships for a Happy Life ... 74

Practical Takeaway: ... 75

   1. Evaluate Your Relationships: ... 75

   2. Balance Career Ambitions with Relationship-Building: ... 76

   3. Communicate Openly with Loved Ones: ... 76

   4. Create Traditions and Rituals: ... 77

Conclusion: Wealth Without Relationships is Empty ... 77

Conclusion: Wealth Wisdom—Mastering the Mindset for Long-Term Success ... 79

   Summary of Key Lessons: ... 79

     1. Wealth is More Than Numbers: ... 79

     2. Patience is a Superpower: ... 79

     3. Emotional Intelligence is Key to Financial Success: ... 80

     4. Discipline and Habits Build Wealth: ... 80

     5. Overcoming Instant Gratification: ... 80

     6. Relationships Are the Real Riches: ... 80

     7. Health is the Greatest Wealth: ... 81

     8. Happiness Can't Be Bought: ... 81

   Call to Action: ... 81

"Wealth Wisdom: Beyond the Balance Sheet"

Your Next Steps: 82
Final Thought: 83

Introduction: Redefining Wealth

When you think of wealth, what's the first thing that comes to mind? Most of us immediately picture money, financial assets, maybe a large house, a luxury car, or a successful career. In our society, wealth is often defined by these material markers—the size of our bank accounts or the status symbols we accumulate. And while these things are important for financial security, wealth goes far beyond the numbers.

Wealth, in its truest form, isn't just about how much money you have. It's about how you live your life, how you balance your ambitions with your happiness, how you manage your time, relationships, and health alongside your financial goals. The richest people are not always the ones with the most money; they are often the ones who have mastered the art of balancing financial success with emotional well-being, meaningful relationships, and a sense of personal fulfillment.

In this book, we're going to redefine wealth. We'll explore how behavior, discipline, and emotional intelligence are the real drivers behind long-term financial success. But more importantly, we'll dive into the idea that true wealth is about living a balanced, fulfilling life, not just a financially abundant one.

The Emotional Price of Financial Success

Let me tell you a story.

I once knew a man who, on paper, was the epitome of success. He had built a business from the ground up and turned it into a multimillion-dollar company. His life was filled with the luxuries most people dream of: a sprawling house, luxury cars, expensive vacations. He had the financial wealth that many spend their lives striving for.

But despite all this, he was deeply unhappy. His marriage was strained, his children barely spoke to him, and he was constantly stressed, anxious, and battling health issues. He told me once, "I thought if I made enough money, everything else would fall into place. But the more I made, the more I realized that the things I neglected—my relationships, my health, my peace of mind—are the things that truly matter."

This man's story is not unique. So many people chase financial success with the belief that once they reach a certain number, everything else will magically align. But as we'll see throughout this book, financial success without balance often leads to disillusionment, stress, and a profound sense of emptiness.

The Hidden Side of Wealth

This book is not just about how to manage your money or grow your wealth—though those are certainly important. Instead, we're going to explore the hidden side of wealth: the mindset, discipline, and emotional intelligence that shape not only our financial success but also our overall sense of fulfillment.

We'll look at how people often sabotage their own financial goals through emotional spending, poor decision-making, and short-term thinking. We'll discuss the importance of patience, resilience, and long-term thinking in building lasting wealth. And we'll emphasize the critical truth that wealth without health, happiness, or strong relationships is empty.

The goal of this book is to help you redefine what wealth means to you, and to give you the tools to not just grow your financial assets, but to cultivate a life that feels truly rich—emotionally, mentally, and relationally.

As you read through the chapters, I invite you to reflect on your own life and financial journey. Are you pursuing wealth at the cost of your well-being? Are your financial decisions aligned with your personal values and long-term goals? Together, we'll explore how mastering your mindset and behavior can lead to both financial prosperity and personal fulfillment.

This is a book about more than money. It's about living a life of true wealth. Let's begin the journey.

"Wealth Wisdom: Beyond the Balance Sheet"

Part 1: The Mindset for Wealth

Chapter 1: Patience is the Ultimate Wealth Strategy

When it comes to building wealth, there's one virtue that stands above all others: patience. In a world that thrives on instant gratification—where you can order anything with a click, stream entire TV series in one sitting, or receive next-day delivery—it's no surprise that the concept of patience feels outdated. But when it comes to financial success, patience isn't just a nice-to-have trait; it's an essential strategy.

The Power of Patience and Delayed Gratification

Patience is the foundation of long-term wealth. It's what keeps you from pulling out your investments at the first sign of market fluctuation. It's what prevents you from spending your savings on a short-term luxury when that money could be working for you in the long run. Yet, patience is one of the hardest disciplines to master because our brains are hardwired to crave immediate rewards.

In this chapter, we'll explore why patience is not only a critical wealth strategy but why mastering it can mean the difference between a lifetime of financial struggle and long-term prosperity.

The Marshmallow Test and Its Wealth Implications

Let's start with one of the most famous psychological studies that illustrates the power of patience—the marshmallow test. In the late 1960s, psychologist Walter Mischel conducted an experiment where young children were given a choice: they could eat one marshmallow immediately, or wait 15 minutes and receive two marshmallows instead. Some children waited, others didn't. But what's more interesting is what happened years later.

Follow-up studies revealed that the children who were able to delay gratification had better life outcomes, including higher SAT scores, lower levels of substance abuse, and better social skills. More importantly for our purposes, they had better financial habits. What this study teaches us is that the ability to wait for greater rewards is a key indicator of future success—not just in life, but in wealth-building as well.

In the world of personal finance, patience translates directly to your ability to save, invest, and let your money grow over time. This is where the concept of *compound interest* becomes crucial.

The Power of Compound Interest

Albert Einstein is often credited with saying, "Compound interest is the eighth wonder of the world. He who understands it, earns it; he who doesn't, pays it." Whether or not Einstein actually said this, the wisdom behind the quote is undeniable. Compound interest is the process by which your investment grows not just based on your initial principal, but also on the accumulated interest over time.

The key to making compound interest work for you? Time and patience. The longer you leave your money invested, the more it grows, and the more you benefit from this compounding effect. Yet, many people give up too soon. They expect rapid gains, and when they don't see immediate results, they pull their money out or switch strategies. But the truth is, the greatest rewards from compound interest often come after years—sometimes decades—of patient investing.

Examples of Patience in Action

Let's look at a few real-world examples to highlight how patience pays off when building wealth.

Take Warren Buffett, one of the wealthiest people in the world, often hailed as the Oracle of Omaha. While Buffett made his first investment at the age of 11, most of his wealth came later in life. In fact, Buffett didn't become a billionaire until his 50s. Why? Because he followed a disciplined investment strategy, relying on compound interest and the power of time. Buffett is the perfect example of how patience, combined with sound financial decisions, is the ultimate wealth-building strategy.

Another story involves Grace Groner, a woman who lived a relatively simple life, working as a secretary for a pharmaceutical company. When Grace passed away in 2010, it was discovered that her estate was worth $7 million. How did she do it? Grace purchased three shares of stock in her company in 1935 and never sold them.

Over the years, with patience and the power of compounding, her modest investment grew into a fortune.

These stories aren't about being born into wealth or having access to complex financial strategies. They are about discipline and, most importantly, patience.

Practical Takeaway: How to Cultivate Patience in Your Financial Life

So, how do you incorporate patience into your own financial strategy? How do you resist the urge for immediate gratification and instead focus on long-term growth? Here are a few practical steps you can take:

1. **Set Long-Term Goals:** The first step in cultivating patience is having a clear vision of where you want to be financially in the long run. Whether it's saving for retirement, purchasing a home, or achieving financial independence, having a long-term goal helps anchor your short-term decisions. Every time you're tempted to spend or pull out an investment, remind yourself of the bigger picture.
2. **Break It Down:** While long-term goals are essential, they can sometimes feel overwhelming or distant. Break your long-term goals into smaller, manageable milestones. For example, if your goal is to save $100,000, set smaller benchmarks like saving $10,000 within the next year. Celebrating these smaller achievements will keep you motivated and remind you that progress is being made.

3. **Automate Your Savings and Investments:** One of the best ways to remove the temptation to spend is to automate your savings and investment contributions. Set up automatic transfers from your checking account to your savings or investment accounts each month. This way, you're building wealth passively without constantly having to make decisions about whether to save or spend.
4. **Visualize the Future:** Sometimes, it's hard to be patient because the future feels abstract. Try visualizing what your life will look like when you reach your financial goals. Imagine how much more comfortable, secure, and free you'll feel knowing you've built a solid financial foundation. Keep this vision in mind when short-term distractions arise.
5. **Track Your Progress:** It's easy to get discouraged if you don't see progress right away. One way to stay motivated is by tracking your progress regularly. Even if the gains are small, watching your wealth grow—slowly but surely—can reinforce the value of patience.

Conclusion: Wealth is Built Over Time, Not Overnight

Patience is a skill, and like any skill, it can be developed. The more you practice patience in your financial life, the more natural it will become. Remember, wealth is not built overnight. The true wealth-building process requires time, consistency, and discipline.

By understanding the importance of delayed gratification and staying focused on the long-term benefits of patient investing, you can avoid many of the traps that lead to financial failure. Patience is the ultimate wealth strategy because, in the end, it's not about getting rich quickly—it's about staying rich for life.

In the following chapters, we'll continue to explore other critical mindsets that help shape not only financial success but also a life of balance, happiness, and fulfillment. But remember this: the path to wealth isn't a sprint—it's a marathon, and patience is what will see you to the finish line.

Chapter 2: Emotional Intelligence in Wealth Management

When we talk about managing wealth, most people immediately think of numbers, strategies, and knowledge. They think of stock market trends, budgeting techniques, and investment portfolios. But there's another, often overlooked, factor that plays a crucial role in financial success—**emotional intelligence (EQ)**. In fact, your ability to manage your emotions may be even more important than your ability to crunch numbers.

The Power of Emotional Intelligence in Financial Success

Emotional intelligence, often described as the ability to understand, manage, and regulate your emotions, is one of the most powerful tools you can have in wealth management. Why? Because in the financial world, emotions like fear, greed, anxiety, and excitement can easily cloud judgment. Decisions driven by these emotions can lead to impulsive actions, from panic-selling stocks during a market crash to overspending in the pursuit of happiness.

If wealth-building were purely a numbers game, we'd all just follow the formulas for success. But as we know, life—and finance—is much more complicated than that. Emotional intelligence helps you navigate the emotional ups and downs of wealth management, allowing you to make rational decisions even in the most stressful situations.

Emotional Intelligence and Decision-Making

In the world of finance, being smart is important, but being emotionally intelligent is essential. Let's break down why emotional intelligence matters so much, particularly in decision-making.

How Emotional Intelligence Affects Financial Decisions

Think of a time when the stock market was in free fall or when you had an unexpected expense that felt overwhelming. Did you react calmly, or did you panic? For many people, periods of uncertainty trigger strong emotional responses—responses that can lead to poor decisions. Here are some common ways that emotions like fear, greed, and anxiety influence financial decisions:

- **Fear:** During market downturns or economic crises, fear is one of the most common emotions. Fear can lead to panic-selling investments, liquidating assets, or making hasty financial moves without a clear plan. In these moments, many people feel compelled to act out of fear of losing everything, when, in reality, staying the course or re-evaluating calmly might have been the better strategy.
- **Greed:** On the flip side of fear is greed. During market booms or periods of high growth, greed can blind people to risks. How often have we heard stories of investors putting all their money into a "hot stock" or a "sure thing," only to lose it all when the market corrects? Greed can lead to

overconfidence, unrealistic expectations, and poor risk management.
- **Anxiety:** Financial decisions are often accompanied by a sense of anxiety, especially when we're not sure of the outcome. Anxiety can lead to indecision—choosing not to act at all—or making rushed decisions simply to feel a sense of control. In the long term, anxiety-driven financial behaviors can sabotage your wealth-building efforts, leading to underinvestment or poor savings habits.

Emotions and Market Volatility

Let's consider how emotional intelligence plays out during periods of market volatility. The stock market, for instance, is famous for its unpredictable ups and downs. For investors, the rollercoaster ride of prices can cause emotional turmoil. When markets are thriving, people may feel euphoric, invincible even. But when the market dips, panic sets in.

Many novice investors make the mistake of buying high—when everyone is talking about how great the market is—and selling low, when the news is filled with doom and gloom. Why does this happen? Because they are letting emotions dictate their actions rather than a sound investment strategy.

Emotionally intelligent investors, however, stay calm. They've developed the self-awareness to recognize the emotions they're feeling and the discipline to stick to their long-term plan, regardless of the market's fluctuations.

Stories of Emotion-Driven Financial Choices

To see this in action, let's look at a few real-life examples of people whose financial decisions were derailed by their emotions.

The Panic Seller

Meet Sarah, a young professional who had been diligently investing in her 401(k) for years. She had a diversified portfolio and was excited about building long-term wealth. But when the market dropped suddenly during an economic downturn, Sarah panicked. She watched the news constantly, overwhelmed by reports of economic collapse. Fearful of losing all her savings, she sold off a significant portion of her investments at the lowest point.

Within months, the market rebounded, and Sarah regretted her decision. Had she stayed calm and kept her investments, she would have recovered her losses and even seen gains. Instead, she locked in her losses because she let fear drive her choices.

The Overconfident Investor

On the other side of the spectrum is Mark, a successful entrepreneur who had seen his business thrive. Flush with cash, Mark began dabbling in stock market investments. He struck gold with a couple of early investments, which only fueled his confidence. Feeling invincible, he started making bigger, riskier bets on the market, often ignoring the advice of his financial advisor.

When the market corrected, Mark lost a substantial portion of his wealth. His greed and overconfidence led him to take unnecessary risks, and he paid the price for not keeping his emotions in check.

Both of these stories show the consequences of emotional decision-making and how developing emotional intelligence could have led to better outcomes.

Practical Takeaway: Strategies to Boost Your Emotional Intelligence in Financial Decisions

So how do you avoid letting your emotions get the best of you when it comes to money? The answer lies in cultivating emotional intelligence. Here are a few strategies that can help you make more mindful, rational financial decisions:

1. Practice Self-Awareness

The first step to mastering emotional intelligence is becoming aware of your emotions. The next time you're about to make a financial decision—whether it's an investment, a major purchase, or even an everyday spending choice—pause and check in with yourself. What are you feeling? Is it fear? Excitement? Anxiety? Simply acknowledging your emotions can give you the distance you need to make a more rational choice.

2. Develop Mindfulness

Mindfulness is the practice of being present in the moment without judgment. When applied to financial decisions, mindfulness helps you separate your emotions from your actions. If you're feeling anxious about money, for example, take a moment to breathe, ground yourself, and reflect on your long-term goals. Mindfulness practices like meditation can also help you build resilience to stress and anxiety.

3. Set Rules for Yourself

Pre-commitment strategies are a great way to outsmart your emotions. For example, set a rule that you will not make any major financial decisions when you're feeling overly emotional—whether you're elated or upset. Similarly, create a plan for your investments and commit to following that plan no matter what the market does. By setting rules in advance, you can avoid making impulsive decisions in the heat of the moment.

4. Seek Outside Perspectives

When emotions are high, it can be hard to see the situation clearly. This is where a trusted advisor or a second opinion can make all the difference. Whether it's a financial advisor, a friend, or a mentor, having someone to provide a calm, outside perspective can help you stay grounded and focused on your long-term goals.

5. Focus on the Long-Term

Finally, remember that wealth-building is a marathon, not a sprint. When fear or greed threatens to influence your decisions, remind yourself of your long-term vision. Financial success is built over time, and sticking to your strategy through thick and thin is what ultimately leads to lasting wealth.

Conclusion: Emotional Intelligence—The Hidden Superpower in Wealth Management

In the world of wealth management, intelligence and strategy are important, but emotional intelligence is often the hidden superpower that separates successful investors from the rest. By mastering your emotions, cultivating self-awareness, and making decisions from a place of calm, rational thought, you can avoid the pitfalls of emotional decision-making and stay on track toward your financial goals.

In the next chapter, we'll explore how our sense of identity and personal narratives influence our financial choices and how you can reshape your money story to align with your long-term goals. But for now, remember this: the key to mastering wealth is not just understanding the numbers—it's mastering yourself.

Chapter 3: Self-Sabotage—How We Get in Our Own Way

When it comes to building wealth, we're often our own worst enemy. While we like to believe that we make rational financial decisions, the truth is that many of us engage in behaviors that undermine our success. These behaviors often stem from deep-rooted psychological patterns—internal conflicts, limiting beliefs, and unresolved emotional issues that cause us to sabotage our financial progress.

Overcoming Self-Sabotage in Wealth Management

Self-sabotage in personal finance is more common than we might think. Whether it's overspending, procrastinating on financial planning, or making impulsive investment decisions, these behaviors don't just happen out of nowhere. They're often the result of deeper, internal conflicts and fears that we may not even be fully aware of.

This chapter is about uncovering the hidden forces that drive us to undermine our own financial goals—and, more importantly, how to stop them.

Understanding Self-Sabotage and Its Roots

To understand how self-sabotage affects wealth-building, we need to look at the underlying psychological and emotional triggers that cause these behaviors. Self-sabotage isn't just about making bad decisions. It's about making decisions that go against our own best interests, despite knowing better. Let's explore the key factors behind self-sabotage in financial life.

1. Examples of Self-Sabotage in Wealth Management

We've all heard stories of people who seem to be doing well financially, only to fall into destructive patterns that erase their progress. Here are some common examples of self-sabotage in personal finance:

- **Overspending:** Despite knowing the importance of budgeting and saving, many people consistently overspend, often on things they don't need. Whether it's splurging on luxury items or buying on impulse, overspending is a classic form of self-sabotage that keeps people from achieving financial stability.
- **Avoiding Financial Planning:** Procrastination is another common form of self-sabotage. Many individuals avoid looking at their finances, delay saving for retirement, or put off making a budget. Avoidance stems from a deeper fear of confronting financial realities, even when action is necessary for long-term success.
- **Impulsive Investment Decisions:** Some individuals, driven by greed or impatience, make impulsive investments, chasing "hot" trends or reacting emotionally to market news. These decisions are rarely based on solid research or strategy and often lead to significant financial losses.
- **Under-Earning or Fear of Success:** On the flip side, some people self-sabotage by undercharging for their services, avoiding opportunities for

growth, or feeling uncomfortable with the idea of accumulating wealth. This often comes from a fear of success, where financial prosperity feels unfamiliar or "undeserved."

2. The Psychological Roots of Self-Sabotage

Why do we sabotage our financial goals, even when we know better? The answer lies in the complex world of psychology. Here are a few common reasons:

- **Fear of Success:** Success brings change, and change can be uncomfortable. Some individuals subconsciously fear success because they associate it with losing their current identity, facing higher expectations, or stepping out of their comfort zone. This can manifest as avoiding opportunities that would bring financial prosperity.
- **Limiting Beliefs About Money:** Many of us carry subconscious beliefs about money that we developed during childhood or through past experiences. For instance, if you grew up believing that "money is the root of all evil" or that "rich people are selfish," you may unconsciously sabotage your own financial progress to avoid the guilt associated with having wealth.
- **Low Self-Worth:** If someone feels they are undeserving of financial success or happiness, they may sabotage their efforts by making poor decisions that reinforce their internal belief system. For example, someone with low self-worth might overspend as a way to seek external validation or approval through material possessions.

- **Past Trauma or Emotional Baggage:** Unresolved emotional issues or trauma can affect our financial decisions. People who have experienced financial instability or emotional pain related to money might make irrational decisions based on fear or emotional scars, even when they know these actions are harmful.

3. How Past Experiences Shape Our Relationship with Money

The way we relate to money is often shaped by early experiences—whether positive or negative. Did you grow up in a household where money was always a source of stress? Did your family experience financial insecurity or significant debt? Or perhaps you were raised to believe that financial success equals self-worth.

These formative experiences leave lasting impressions on how we handle money as adults. For example:

- **Financial Trauma:** If you grew up in a financially unstable environment, you may develop a scarcity mindset, where you're constantly worried about money even if you're financially secure. This fear can drive hoarding behavior, chronic underspending, or an unwillingness to invest in yourself or your future.
- **Overcompensation:** On the other hand, individuals who grew up in financially deprived households may swing to the opposite extreme. They might overspend as adults, buying things they couldn't have in childhood, or using material

wealth to prove their success to themselves and others.
- **Inherited Beliefs:** Many of us unconsciously carry our parents' beliefs about money into our own lives. If you were raised in a household that valued frugality and hard work, you might internalize those beliefs as an adult. Alternatively, if you grew up in a household where money was used as a measure of success, you may feel driven to accumulate wealth as a way to validate your worth.

Practical Takeaway: How to Overcome Self-Sabotage and Build Healthy Financial Habits

Overcoming self-sabotage requires a combination of self-awareness, emotional healing, and practical steps. Here's how you can begin to break the cycle and create healthier financial behaviors:

1. Identify Your Self-Sabotaging Habits

The first step to breaking free from self-sabotage is recognizing the patterns that are holding you back. Take a moment to reflect on your financial habits. Do you notice a pattern of overspending? Do you tend to procrastinate when it comes to saving or investing?

Exercise: Write down the specific financial behaviors that you know are sabotaging your goals. Be honest with yourself—this isn't about judgment, but about identifying the problem so you can address it.

2. Dig Deeper into the Root Cause

Once you've identified your self-sabotaging habits, the next step is to dig deeper into *why* these behaviors exist. Are you afraid of success? Do you believe that money is inherently "bad"? Are you trying to avoid financial responsibility because it feels overwhelming?

Exercise: For each habit you identified, ask yourself, "What am I afraid of?" or "What past experience might be influencing this behavior?" Uncovering the root cause of your behavior will help you address it at its source.

3. Reframe Limiting Beliefs

If you find that limiting beliefs about money are driving your self-sabotage, it's time to reframe those beliefs. Instead of thinking, "I don't deserve to be wealthy," shift to, "I am capable of creating financial abundance and using it for good." Reframing helps you replace negative, limiting beliefs with empowering ones.

Exercise: Write down your old, limiting beliefs about money and replace each one with a new, positive affirmation. Repeat these affirmations daily to reinforce your new mindset.

4. Build Healthy Financial Habits

Finally, it's important to replace self-sabotaging behaviors with healthy financial habits. If you struggle with overspending, create a budget and stick to it. If you avoid investing because of fear, start with small, low-risk investments to build confidence. The key is to take small, consistent steps that align with your long-term financial goals.

Exercise: Choose one self-sabotaging behavior to focus on this month. Create a plan for how you will replace that behavior with a healthy habit, and track your progress daily or weekly.

Conclusion: Mastering Your Inner Game of Wealth

Self-sabotage can feel like an invisible force holding you back from financial success, but it doesn't have to be. By bringing awareness to your habits, understanding the emotional roots behind your behaviors, and taking small, actionable steps toward healthier choices, you can overcome self-sabotage and unlock your true potential for wealth-building.

In the next chapter, we'll explore how cultivating patience can be one of the most powerful wealth-building strategies of all—and how resisting the lure of instant gratification can lead to lasting financial success.

Part 2: Building a Strong Wealth Foundation

Chapter 4: Discipline—The Foundation of Wealth

When it comes to building and maintaining wealth, there's one trait that stands above all others: **discipline**. No matter how intelligent or lucky you are, without discipline, even the best financial plans will eventually crumble. Discipline is what keeps you on track during tough times, prevents you from chasing short-term pleasures at the expense of long-term success, and ensures that your wealth-building efforts stand the test of time.

Discipline as the Cornerstone of Wealth-Building

In this chapter, we'll explore why discipline is the true foundation of wealth. It's not just about sticking to a budget or resisting impulse buys—discipline is the mindset that enables you to make consistent, wise financial choices, day after day, year after year.

Let's dig deeper into how discipline manifests in budgeting, saving, and investing, and why it's often the difference between financial success and failure.

Understanding the Role of Discipline in Wealth

1. The Importance of Financial Discipline in Budgeting, Saving, and Investing

Discipline is required at every stage of wealth-building. Whether you're creating a budget, saving for future goals, or making long-term investments, your ability to remain disciplined will determine your success.

- **Budgeting:** Having a budget is essential, but sticking to it requires discipline. It's easy to go off track when faced with temptations—whether it's a fancy dinner, a weekend getaway, or the latest gadget. However, financial discipline means consistently prioritizing your needs and long-term goals over momentary desires.
- **Saving:** Consistent saving is a hallmark of disciplined wealth-builders. While some may wait for an ideal moment to start saving, disciplined individuals save regularly, even if it's a modest amount. They understand that the key to accumulating wealth is consistency, not perfection.
- **Investing:** The same principle applies to investing. Whether it's the temptation to pull money out of the market during downturns or the allure of chasing quick profits, disciplined investors know that wealth-building is a marathon, not a sprint. They stick to their investment strategy and let compound interest work its magic over time.

2. Stories of Individuals Who Built Wealth Slowly But Steadily Through Discipline

Throughout history, many individuals have built significant wealth—not through sudden windfalls or speculative investments, but through a steady, disciplined approach. Let's look at a few examples:

- **Warren Buffett**: Often called the greatest investor of all time, Buffett's strategy isn't glamorous, but it's rooted in discipline. He follows a simple philosophy: buy good companies at a reasonable price and hold them for the long term. Buffett's wealth didn't come from quick wins but from disciplined, patient investing over decades.
- **A Modest Saver Who Became a Millionaire**: Take the story of Grace Groner, a secretary who worked at Abbott Laboratories for over 40 years. Grace didn't have a lavish lifestyle, but she was incredibly disciplined with her money. She invested in Abbott stock and held onto it for decades, allowing it to compound. Upon her death, she left a legacy of over $7 million to charity—all built through simple, disciplined investing.
- **Everyday People Avoiding Lifestyle Inflation**: Many people who achieve financial success fall prey to *lifestyle inflation*—the tendency to increase spending as income rises. However, disciplined individuals resist this temptation. They maintain their frugal habits and continue to save or invest the difference, allowing their wealth to grow steadily. These individuals understand that wealth is not about how much you earn, but how much you keep and invest over time.

3. The Short-Term Pleasures of Spending vs. The Long-Term Rewards of Discipline

Spending money on short-term pleasures can feel great in the moment, but it often leads to regret later on. Buying that luxury car, going on extravagant vacations, or splurging on the latest tech gadget might provide a temporary boost in happiness, but those moments are fleeting. Over time, the thrill fades, and you're left with depleted savings or mounting debt.

On the other hand, discipline might not feel as exciting in the short term, but the long-term rewards are immense. By consistently saving, investing, and living within your means, you set yourself up for financial freedom—where you no longer have to worry about money, and you have the flexibility to live life on your own terms.

It's important to recognize that discipline is not about denying yourself joy or pleasure. It's about making conscious, deliberate choices that align with your long-term goals. The reward is not just financial security but the peace of mind that comes from knowing you are in control of your financial future.

Practical Takeaway: How to Cultivate Financial Discipline

Now that we've seen how powerful financial discipline can be, let's focus on how you can cultivate it in your own life. Building discipline doesn't happen overnight—it's a gradual process that requires consistency and commitment. Here are some practical strategies to help you develop and maintain financial discipline:

1. Automate Your Savings and Investments

One of the best ways to ensure you save consistently is to automate the process. Set up automatic transfers to your savings or investment accounts so that a portion of your income is saved before you even have a chance to spend it. By removing the need for willpower, automation makes saving effortless.

Tip: Many financial experts recommend starting with 10-20% of your income, but the key is to start where you can and increase the amount over time.

2. Set Realistic Budgets

A budget is a critical tool for financial discipline, but it needs to be realistic. If your budget is too restrictive, you're likely to abandon it. Instead, create a budget that allows for some flexibility while still prioritizing your savings goals.

Tip: Use the 50/30/20 rule as a guideline: allocate 50% of your income for necessities, 30% for discretionary spending, and 20% for savings and debt repayment.

3. Build Habits Through Routines

Discipline is often about creating routines and sticking to them. Whether it's reviewing your budget weekly, setting aside time to track your investments, or planning your meals to avoid impulsive spending, routines help reinforce disciplined behavior.

Tip: Use a financial planner or app to track your spending and savings goals. By regularly reviewing your progress, you'll stay accountable and motivated.

4. Break Goals into Small, Manageable Milestones

Building wealth can seem overwhelming, especially if you have big financial goals. To maintain discipline, break your larger goals into smaller, manageable milestones. Celebrate each milestone as you reach it, and use these wins to build momentum.

Tip: If your goal is to save $50,000, break it down into monthly or yearly targets, such as saving $500 per month. This makes the goal feel more achievable and helps you stay focused.

5. Focus on Your "Why"

Finally, remember why you're building wealth in the first place. Whether it's financial independence, providing for your family, or enjoying a comfortable retirement, keeping your "why" in mind will help you stay disciplined when temptations arise.

Tip: Write down your financial goals and the reasons behind them. Keep this list somewhere visible to remind yourself of your long-term vision whenever you're tempted to stray.

Conclusion: The Power of Discipline in Wealth-Building

Discipline is the bedrock of long-term financial success. Without it, even the most sophisticated financial plans can fall apart. With it, you have the foundation needed to build lasting wealth—no matter your starting point.

As you move forward, remember that discipline is not about depriving yourself. It's about making deliberate choices that align with your long-term vision of success. Every time you choose discipline over short-term pleasure, you're investing in your future self.

In the next chapter, we'll dive deeper into the role of emotional intelligence in wealth-building and how mastering your emotions can help you make better financial decisions.

Chapter 5: Overcoming Instant Gratification

In today's fast-paced world, the allure of instant gratification is everywhere. From one-click online shopping to the dopamine rush of social media notifications, we live in a society that rewards immediacy. We're constantly bombarded with messages that encourage us to "buy now," "treat yourself," and enjoy things without waiting. While this can be fun in the moment, it's often at odds with the slow, deliberate process of building wealth. In this chapter, we'll explore why humans are wired for instant gratification, how it sabotages long-term financial success, and what we can do to overcome these impulses in favor of a wealth-building mindset.

Resisting Instant Gratification in a Culture of Now

The key theme here is the conflict between the human desire for immediate rewards and the disciplined patience required for wealth-building. We will discuss the psychology behind instant gratification and how it's deeply embedded in our behaviors. But more importantly, we'll explore strategies that help shift this mindset toward long-term financial health and success.

Understanding Instant Gratification and Its Impact on Wealth

1. Why Humans Are Wired for Instant Gratification

From an evolutionary standpoint, humans are hardwired for instant gratification. Our ancestors lived in environments where immediate rewards—like food, shelter, and safety—were crucial for survival. In those times, delaying gratification could mean missing out on resources or opportunities. As a result, the brain developed a natural preference for immediate rewards over long-term benefits.

However, in today's world, this wiring can often work against us—especially when it comes to finances. The ability to delay gratification is essential for building wealth, yet it's something we struggle with, as evidenced by credit card debt, low savings rates, and impulsive spending habits.

Research Insight: Studies show that people who can delay gratification tend to experience more success in life, including greater financial stability. The famous *Stanford marshmallow experiment* demonstrated this well: children who were able to resist eating a marshmallow for a period of time (in order to receive two marshmallows later) tended to achieve better life outcomes years down the line. This same principle applies to wealth-building—those who can wait for future rewards by delaying impulsive spending build more stable financial futures.

2. The Cost of Instant Gratification—How It Leads to Debt and Financial Trouble

Instant gratification often leads people to make financial decisions that feel good in the moment but have negative consequences in the long run. Impulse buys, shopping sprees, or even taking on high-interest loans to fund an immediate desire are common examples of how people fall into financial trouble. The ease with which we can access credit, combined with the societal push to "live in the now," makes resisting these temptations even harder.

Let's take a closer look at the ripple effects of instant gratification:

- **Credit Card Debt**: Credit cards make it easy to buy now and worry about paying later. The problem is that "later" comes with high interest rates, and debt quickly accumulates. Many people find themselves stuck in a cycle of debt because they couldn't resist the temptation of an immediate purchase.
- **Lifestyle Inflation**: As people earn more money, they tend to upgrade their lifestyle—bigger homes, nicer cars, more expensive vacations. This "keeping up with the Joneses" mentality is another form of instant gratification that can prevent people from saving and investing for the future.
- **Poor Savings Habits**: Instant gratification also impacts our ability to save. Instead of putting money into a savings account or retirement fund, we're often tempted to spend it on the latest gadget, a new outfit, or an impromptu dinner out. This leaves little room for building a financial safety net or growing wealth through investments.

3. Case Studies of People Who Overcame Instant Gratification and Built Lasting Wealth

Let's look at a few examples of individuals who recognized the pitfalls of instant gratification, shifted their mindset, and ultimately built lasting wealth.

- **Case Study 1: The Story of Sarah—Escaping the Debt Trap**
  Sarah, a young professional, found herself deeply in credit card debt due to her tendency to use shopping as a form of stress relief. She would buy new clothes, gadgets, and take frequent trips, all while ignoring the mounting debt on her credit cards. Eventually, the stress of the debt outweighed the satisfaction of her purchases, and she realized she needed to change. Sarah started by setting small, achievable financial goals—paying off one credit card at a time—and used the "snowball method" to gain momentum. She also implemented a 48-hour rule for big purchases, forcing herself to wait two days before buying anything over a certain price. This simple habit helped her curb impulsive spending and refocus on her long-term financial goals.
- **Case Study 2: The Story of Mark—Trading Short-Term Luxuries for Long-Term Wealth**
  Mark was a high-earning executive who always treated himself to luxury items—designer watches, high-end cars, and lavish vacations. However, despite his six-figure salary, he wasn't saving nearly enough for retirement. Realizing that his current lifestyle wasn't sustainable, Mark made a conscious decision to downsize his life. He sold his expensive car, moved into a more modest home, and redirected the money he saved into

investments. By trading his short-term luxuries for long-term investments, Mark was able to grow his wealth and secure his financial future.

Practical Takeaway: How to Shift Your Mindset from Instant Gratification to Long-Term Success

It's clear that resisting the pull of instant gratification is key to building lasting wealth. But how do you shift your mindset and break free from the cycle of impulsive decisions? Here are a few practical strategies to help you cultivate delayed gratification and prioritize long-term financial success:

1. Create a "Pause Button" for Purchases

Before making any non-essential purchase, implement a mandatory waiting period—such as 48 hours or even a week. This allows you time to reflect on whether the purchase aligns with your financial goals or if it's just an emotional reaction. Often, you'll find that the desire fades over time, and you'll avoid unnecessary spending.

Tip: If you're tempted to make a big purchase, ask yourself, "Will this item bring lasting value, or is it something I'll forget about in a few months?" This question helps you focus on meaningful purchases rather than impulsive ones.

2. Visualize Your Long-Term Financial Goals

One of the best ways to combat instant gratification is to keep your long-term financial goals in mind. Whether it's buying a home, retiring comfortably, or building a financial legacy for your family, visualizing these goals can help you stay disciplined. When you're tempted by a short-term reward, remind yourself of the bigger picture and how saving or investing today will bring greater rewards in the future.

Tip: Create a vision board or a written list of your financial goals and place it somewhere you'll see every day. This visual reminder will reinforce your commitment to long-term wealth-building.

3. Build Rewards for Delayed Gratification

While delayed gratification requires sacrifice, it doesn't mean you should deprive yourself entirely. Build in small rewards along the way to keep yourself motivated. For example, if you meet a savings goal, treat yourself to something modest as a celebration of your progress. This keeps you focused on long-term goals while still enjoying the journey.

Tip: Set up financial milestones—such as saving a certain amount or paying off a specific debt—and reward yourself with a meaningful but controlled treat once you reach those milestones. This helps you associate the act of saving with positive reinforcement.

4. Focus on Experiences, Not Things

Research has shown that people tend to derive more lasting happiness from experiences than from material possessions. Instead of spending money on fleeting material goods, invest in experiences that create lasting memories—like traveling, spending time with loved ones, or pursuing personal growth opportunities.

Tip: Allocate a portion of your budget toward experiences that enrich your life, whether it's learning a new skill, traveling to a new place, or simply enjoying time with friends and family. These experiences offer lasting fulfillment without the clutter or financial strain of material goods.

Conclusion: Mastering the Urge for Instant Gratification

Overcoming instant gratification is one of the biggest challenges in building wealth, but it's also one of the most rewarding. By learning to delay short-term pleasures in favor of long-term rewards, you're not just improving your financial situation—you're developing a mindset that can help you succeed in all areas of life.

Remember, wealth-building is a marathon, not a sprint. The more you can resist the urge for instant gratification and focus on the bigger picture, the more likely you are to achieve lasting financial success. In the next chapter, we'll explore how discipline is not just a tool for saving money, but a foundation for wealth creation across all aspects of life.

Chapter 6: The Role of Habits in Financial Success

When we think of wealth, we often picture grand gestures: making a big investment, landing a lucrative deal, or receiving a substantial raise. But the truth is, wealth isn't built in a single moment. It's created over time through consistent, small habits. In this chapter, we'll dive into the concept of financial habits, how they shape your wealth-building journey, and why the smallest actions can have the greatest impact in the long run.

Wealth is a Result of Consistent Habits

The main idea here is that long-term financial success is rarely the product of one or two major financial decisions. Instead, it's a result of the small, repeated actions you take each day, week, and month. These habits, when compounded over time, create lasting wealth and financial stability.

The Power of Small Habits and Financial Compounding

1. The Power of Compounding—In Both Finance and Behavior

We've all heard about the power of compound interest—the idea that the longer your money stays invested, the more it grows, earning interest on interest. But what's often overlooked is that compounding doesn't just apply to money. The habits you form compound over time as well.

Just like a small investment made consistently grows into a large sum, small positive habits around saving, budgeting, and spending lead to massive financial rewards down the road. On the flip side, bad habits—like impulsive spending or failing to save—compound too, often leading to mounting debt or missed financial opportunities.

Example: Let's say you save just $5 a day by skipping an unnecessary expense, like your daily coffee run. At first glance, $5 seems insignificant. But over the course of a year, that small habit results in over $1,800 saved. And if you were to invest that money with even a modest interest rate, over time, those savings would multiply. That's the power of compounding—both in terms of money and behavior.

2. Atomic Habits: Small Changes, Big Results

James Clear, in his bestselling book *Atomic Habits*, emphasizes the idea that small habits, when performed consistently, create profound changes in our lives. The same principle applies to wealth. Wealth is not the result of making one perfect financial decision. It's about making small, smart decisions consistently.

Think of it like this: saving just 1% of your income or cutting one small recurring expense doesn't feel like a significant change. But over months and years, these tiny adjustments add up. That's the essence of wealth-building through habits—small, repeated actions that grow into something substantial over time.

Clear's concept of "atomic habits" is about focusing on manageable, bite-sized actions rather than grand, overwhelming goals. The key to building wealth is not necessarily about setting enormous savings targets or cutting out all unnecessary spending at once—it's about taking incremental steps, consistently.

3. Real-Life Examples of Wealth-Building Habits

To see the power of habits in action, let's look at some real-world examples of people who built wealth through simple, consistent actions.

- **The Saver Who Paid Himself First:** Take the story of John, an average-earning professional. Early in his career, John decided to "pay himself first," a concept where you automatically transfer a portion of your income into savings before paying bills or spending on anything else. John started with a modest 5% of his paycheck and eventually increased it to 20%. This simple habit allowed him to accumulate a substantial retirement nest egg, even though his income was never extraordinarily high. The key was consistency and automating the process, ensuring that saving became a habit rather than an afterthought.
- **The Investor Who Started Small:** Another example is of Sarah, a young professional who began investing by putting a small percentage of her paycheck into an index fund. At first, the returns seemed minimal. But over the years, her small investments grew substantially, thanks to compound interest. By making investing a non-negotiable habit, Sarah was able to build a

significant portfolio without needing to make risky or massive investments all at once.
- **The Family Who Cut Unnecessary Expenses:** Then there's the story of a family who, after reviewing their budget, realized they were spending hundreds of dollars a month on subscription services they rarely used. By cutting these small, unnecessary expenses and redirecting the money into an emergency fund, they managed to save thousands of dollars a year. This small adjustment not only strengthened their financial security but also freed up resources for long-term investments.

Practical Takeaway: Building Small Financial Habits for Long-Term Success

Now that we've seen how powerful small habits can be, how can you start implementing these habits in your own life? Here are some practical ways to begin building the foundation of your financial success:

1. Start with One or Two Small Changes

You don't need to overhaul your entire financial life overnight. In fact, doing too much at once can lead to burnout or frustration. Instead, identify one or two small habits that you can start today.

- **Example:** Commit to saving 1% more of your income or cutting one unnecessary expense this month. It could be as simple as cooking at home more often instead of eating out or canceling a subscription service you rarely use.

2. Automate Your Habits

The easiest way to stick to a financial habit is to automate it. Set up automatic transfers to your savings or investment account so you don't have to rely on willpower alone. This "set it and forget it" strategy ensures that your financial goals are being met without requiring constant effort.

- **Example:** If you're saving for a specific goal, like a vacation or a down payment on a house, set up an automatic transfer from your checking account to a dedicated savings account each month.

3. Track Your Progress

One of the most motivating aspects of habit-building is seeing your progress over time. Use a simple tracking system to monitor your financial habits. This could be as straightforward as marking off each day or week that you stick to your new habit or using an app to track your savings or investment growth.

- **Example:** If your habit is to save an extra $50 each month, track your balance at the end of each month and celebrate small milestones along the way. This positive reinforcement will keep you motivated to continue.

4. Build Positive Reinforcement Into Your Habits

It's important to reward yourself for sticking to your habits, especially in the early stages. You don't have to spend a lot of money on rewards—something as simple as treating yourself to a small experience or enjoying a favorite hobby can reinforce the positive feelings associated with financial discipline.

- **Example:** If you meet a savings goal or stick to your habit for a month, reward yourself with a simple but meaningful experience, like going for a hike, having a special dinner, or spending time on a personal hobby.

Conclusion: Consistency is Key to Financial Success

Building wealth doesn't happen overnight, and it doesn't require making massive financial decisions all at once. Instead, it's the small, consistent habits—the ones you implement every day or every month—that lead to lasting financial success. Whether it's saving a small percentage of your income, investing regularly, or cutting back on unnecessary expenses, the power of these habits is in their ability to compound over time.

Remember, the road to wealth isn't about perfection—it's about persistence. As you move forward in your financial journey, focus on building small habits that align with your long-term goals. These habits, though they may seem minor at first, will ultimately become the foundation of your financial success. And the best part? Once they're ingrained, they require little effort to maintain, allowing you to build wealth effortlessly over time.

Part 3: Beyond the Balance Sheet—True Wealth

Chapter 7: The Happiness Factor— Why Money Isn't Enough

In our pursuit of financial security and success, many of us are driven by the belief that more money will ultimately lead to more happiness. After all, isn't that what we've been taught—money brings freedom, security, and the ability to live the life we want? But if you've ever earned a big bonus or achieved a major financial milestone, you may have noticed that the happiness it brought was often short-lived. That's because true wealth is not just about what's in your bank account—it's about how fulfilled and balanced your life is.

True Wealth Goes Beyond Financial Security

The central theme of this chapter is simple but profound: money, while important for stability and comfort, is not the key to lasting happiness. True wealth is about balance—finding happiness and fulfillment in life, alongside financial success. While financial freedom can remove stress and provide opportunities, it's what we do with that freedom, and how we live our lives, that determines our true wealth.

Why More Money Doesn't Lead to More Happiness

1. The Hedonic Treadmill: Why We Always Want More

Psychologists have a term for the phenomenon where people continuously seek more and more in the hopes of achieving happiness, only to find themselves stuck in a cycle of wanting more once they get it. It's called the **hedonic treadmill**, and it explains why material possessions, raises, or financial windfalls often don't lead to lasting contentment.

The concept is simple: when you experience something new—whether it's a financial gain, a new car, or a luxury vacation—it gives you a temporary boost in happiness. But after a short time, your happiness level returns to where it was before. You adapt to the new reality and, eventually, you want something more or better. This treadmill keeps us constantly chasing after new things, without ever reaching a lasting state of happiness.

Example: Think about someone who buys their dream car. For the first few weeks, they feel a surge of joy every time they drive it. But after a while, the novelty fades, and they're back to feeling the same as before. Soon, they may start looking for the next purchase that will bring them that fleeting joy.

2. Stories of Wealthy Individuals Who Found Happiness Beyond Money

Money alone doesn't guarantee happiness—something we've seen time and again through the stories of individuals who have reached financial success but still felt empty. These people discovered that their wealth didn't fill the emotional or spiritual gaps in their lives, and they had to look elsewhere for true fulfillment.

Take the example of a successful entrepreneur who built a multi-million-dollar business. Despite his financial success, he felt disconnected from his family and overwhelmed by the pressure of maintaining his lifestyle. It wasn't until he took a step back—focusing on his relationships, giving back to his community, and pursuing hobbies he loved—that he found the happiness he had been missing.

On the other hand, there are stories of people with modest means who live rich, fulfilling lives. They may not have millions in the bank, but they've found happiness through meaningful work, strong relationships, and living in alignment with their values. These stories challenge the idea that wealth is synonymous with happiness and show that true wealth is often measured by life satisfaction, not by net worth.

3. Research on Wealth and Happiness: Where's the Tipping Point?

Research on the correlation between wealth and happiness shows that while money does impact happiness up to a certain point, beyond that point, more money has a diminishing effect on life satisfaction. Studies suggest that **once basic needs are met**—things like housing, food, healthcare, and a bit of discretionary income—additional wealth has little impact on overall happiness.

In fact, research from Princeton University's Daniel Kahneman and Angus Deaton found that once people earn around **$75,000 per year** (in the U.S.), additional income doesn't significantly boost their emotional well-being. The study suggests that beyond this threshold, factors like relationships, health, and a sense of purpose have a much greater impact on happiness than extra money.

This tipping point might vary based on location, cost of living, or personal circumstances, but the lesson is clear: after a certain level, chasing more financial wealth won't necessarily bring more happiness. Instead, cultivating non-material aspects of life, like relationships and personal growth, becomes far more important.

Practical Takeaway: Cultivating Happiness Alongside Financial Success

While it's important to pursue financial stability and security, it's equally important to focus on what truly brings happiness and fulfillment in life. Wealth alone won't make you happy—it's how you use that wealth and how you live your life that matters most.

1. Focus on Meaningful Work and Purpose

We spend much of our lives working, and research shows that finding meaning and purpose in our work is a major contributor to happiness. Instead of focusing solely on a high-paying job, consider how your work aligns with your values, passions, and long-term goals.

- **Action Step:** Reflect on what gives you a sense of purpose in your career. If your current job doesn't align with your values or bring you satisfaction, consider small changes you can make to bring more meaning to your work—whether it's finding new challenges, mentoring others, or shifting your focus to work that feels fulfilling.

2. Invest in Relationships

Strong, healthy relationships are one of the most important predictors of long-term happiness. Investing time and energy in nurturing relationships with family, friends, and loved ones often brings more lasting joy than any material purchase.

- **Action Step:** Make relationships a priority. Schedule regular time with loved ones, practice gratitude, and focus on building deeper connections. These relationships will provide emotional support and fulfillment far beyond what money can offer.

3. Pursue Personal Passions

Often, we get so caught up in the pursuit of financial success that we forget to make time for hobbies and personal passions. Whether it's painting, hiking, volunteering, or learning a new skill, engaging in activities that bring you joy can have a profound impact on your well-being.

- **Action Step:** Set aside time each week to engage in something you're passionate about. It doesn't need to be time-consuming or expensive—just something that makes you feel fulfilled and connected to yourself.

4. Practice Gratitude and Mindfulness

Gratitude and mindfulness practices have been shown to increase happiness by shifting your focus from what's lacking to what you already have. By appreciating the present moment and the non-material riches in your life, you can cultivate a deeper sense of contentment.

- **Action Step:** Start a daily gratitude journal, where you write down three things you're thankful for each day. Practicing mindfulness—whether through meditation, mindful eating, or simply being present—can also help you feel more connected and grounded in your day-to-day life.

Conclusion: Wealth with Happiness—A Balanced Approach

In our pursuit of financial wealth, it's easy to lose sight of the things that truly bring happiness and fulfillment. But by focusing on meaningful work, nurturing relationships, and cultivating personal passions, we can create a life that feels rich in every sense of the word. Money is important, yes—but it's not everything.

The key is finding balance. As you continue building your financial future, remember that true wealth isn't just about what's in your bank account—it's about how happy, fulfilled, and balanced your life feels.

Chapter 8: Health and Well-Being—The Greatest Wealth

When we think about wealth, the first image that often comes to mind is money—financial assets, investments, or a high-paying career. But there's a foundational aspect of wealth that is often overlooked, and without it, financial success can feel hollow: **health and well-being**. The saying "health is wealth" may sound cliché, but it's grounded in truth. You could have all the money in the world, but without physical and mental well-being, what good is it?

In this chapter, we're going to explore the profound connection between wealth and health, highlighting how the two must work together to create a truly successful, fulfilling life. Neglecting your well-being in the pursuit of financial success is a short-sighted strategy, one that can leave you wealthy but unhealthy—and ultimately unfulfilled.

Wealth and Well-Being Must Go Hand in Hand

Good health isn't just a "nice-to-have"—it's essential for living a rich and rewarding life. When we neglect our health in favor of professional ambition, the costs can be devastating. Chronic stress, burnout, and unhealthy lifestyle choices don't just take a toll on our bodies; they also impact our ability to enjoy the wealth we've worked so hard to build.

This chapter will focus on why maintaining physical and mental health is one of the most important investments you can make. True wealth includes the energy and vitality to enjoy your life, the peace of mind that comes from being physically well, and the longevity to savor the fruits of your labor.

The Link Between Health and Financial Success

1. The Price of Burnout and Chronic Stress

In the pursuit of financial success, many people sacrifice their health, often without realizing it until it's too late. The grind of long hours, sleepless nights, and constant pressure can lead to burnout, leaving you emotionally drained and physically exhausted. Chronic stress doesn't just impact your mental well-being—it weakens your immune system, increases the risk of heart disease, and can significantly shorten your lifespan.

Example: Think of the high-powered executive who spends decades climbing the corporate ladder. Their income grows, their lifestyle improves, but as the pressure mounts, they find themselves dealing with insomnia, anxiety, and even stress-induced illnesses. In their quest for financial success, they've neglected the one thing that truly matters: their health.

Financial success achieved at the cost of your health is a hollow victory. When you're physically unwell, you can't enjoy the lifestyle that wealth affords. And if your body or mind gives out, your ability to generate more wealth—and to live a meaningful life—diminishes rapidly.

2. Stories of Wealth at the Cost of Health

We've all heard stories of wealthy individuals who, after years of hard work and accumulating vast fortunes, find themselves grappling with major health issues. From entrepreneurs who sacrificed sleep and well-being to build a business, to corporate leaders who developed chronic health conditions from stress, these stories are cautionary tales.

Case Study: Consider the story of a successful entrepreneur who built a multimillion-dollar company. He worked relentlessly, often neglecting sleep, proper nutrition, and exercise. By his late 40s, he was diagnosed with heart disease—a direct result of the stress and lack of self-care. While he had the financial resources to access the best medical care, he found himself spending more time in hospitals than enjoying his wealth. His experience forced him to reassess his priorities and redefine what "success" really meant.

This pattern is all too common. People believe that by sacrificing their health now, they will enjoy it later. But often, the damage is already done, and they are left spending their wealth to recover their health—an endeavor that can take years, if it's even possible at all.

3. Balancing Ambition with Self-Care

Being ambitious and driven toward financial goals is not a bad thing, but it's crucial to balance that ambition with self-care. If you're sacrificing sleep, neglecting exercise, or skipping meals in the name of professional success, it's time to reassess your approach. True wealth is about balance—achieving financial success **without** sacrificing your health and well-being along the way.

Consider the examples of highly successful individuals who prioritize health as part of their wealth strategy. Whether it's billionaires like Richard Branson, who swears by daily exercise, or business moguls like Arianna Huffington, who has become an advocate for the importance of sleep, many of the world's most successful people have learned that without good health, financial success is meaningless.

Practical Takeaway: Integrating Health and Well-Being into Wealth-Building

To build a life of true wealth, it's essential to prioritize your health as much as you prioritize your finances. Here are practical strategies to help you integrate well-being into your wealth-building journey:

1. Manage Stress Proactively

Stress is inevitable, especially when pursuing ambitious goals. However, the key is to manage it before it takes a toll on your health. Incorporate stress-reducing activities into your daily routine—whether it's yoga, meditation, journaling, or simply taking a walk in nature. Learn to recognize the signs of burnout early and take action before it escalates.

- **Action Step:** Dedicate 10-15 minutes each day to a mindfulness practice. Even a brief period of meditation can help reduce stress and improve focus, helping you approach financial challenges with a calm, clear mind.

2. Make Physical Activity Non-Negotiable

Exercise isn't just about staying fit—it's crucial for mental clarity, stress reduction, and long-term health. Make physical activity a non-negotiable part of your daily routine, whether it's hitting the gym, going for a run, or practicing yoga.

- **Action Step:** Set a goal to move your body for at least 30 minutes a day. It could be as simple as a walk during your lunch break or a morning workout before you start your day.

3. Prioritize Sleep

Sleep is often the first thing sacrificed in the pursuit of success, but it's one of the most important pillars of health. Chronic sleep deprivation not only weakens your immune system but also impairs decision-making, which can negatively affect your financial choices.

- **Action Step:** Create a sleep routine that allows for 7-9 hours of quality rest each night. Turn off screens an hour before bed, and ensure your sleep environment is conducive to rest—dark, quiet, and comfortable.

4. Practice Mindful Eating

It's easy to reach for quick, unhealthy meals when you're busy, but your diet plays a significant role in your overall well-being. Prioritize balanced, nutritious meals that fuel your body and mind. Remember, your energy and focus directly impact your ability to succeed financially.

- **Action Step:** Plan your meals for the week to ensure you're eating a balanced diet. Include plenty of fruits, vegetables, lean proteins, and whole grains to support sustained energy levels.

5. Set Health-Related Goals Alongside Financial Goals

When you set your financial goals for the year, don't forget to set health-related goals as well. Whether it's maintaining a healthy weight, reducing stress, or improving your fitness level, setting health goals ensures that your journey to wealth doesn't come at the cost of your well-being.

- **Action Step:** Write down one health goal for the next six months, and treat it with the same importance as your financial goals. Whether it's running a 5K, losing 10 pounds, or lowering your cholesterol, track your progress and celebrate your achievements.

Conclusion: True Wealth is a Balance Between Health and Financial Success

Without your health, your financial success is significantly diminished. True wealth is about balance—it's about achieving your financial goals while maintaining your physical and mental well-being. The journey to wealth should not leave you burned out, stressed, or unhealthy. Instead, it should be a balanced pursuit that leaves you feeling energized, fulfilled, and ready to enjoy the fruits of your labor.

As you work toward building wealth, don't forget to take care of yourself along the way. After all, good health is the greatest wealth of all.

Chapter 9: Relationships—The Currency of Connection

We often hear the phrase, "It's lonely at the top," and for many people, that sentiment rings painfully true. As we chase financial success and professional milestones, it's easy to overlook one of the most critical forms of wealth—**our relationships**. True wealth isn't just measured by the numbers in your bank account but by the quality of the connections you share with others.

In this chapter, we'll explore how the pursuit of wealth can sometimes come at the expense of our relationships, and why maintaining meaningful connections is essential for a balanced, fulfilling life. Wealth without connection can feel hollow, and many who reach financial success realize that it means little without strong personal bonds. Let's redefine what it means to be rich, focusing on the currency of love, friendships, and family ties.

Wealth Means Little Without Strong Relationships

At the core of a fulfilling life are relationships—with family, friends, partners, colleagues, and even communities. The connections we nurture shape our emotional well-being, provide us with support during tough times, and amplify our joy during moments of success. Yet, the modern pursuit of financial gain, career advancement, and material success often leads people to sacrifice these crucial relationships.

We've seen it before: someone devotes years of their life to building a successful business, working long hours, traveling constantly, and rarely spending time with their loved ones. They may become financially rich, but when they finally take a breath, they realize the cost of their success—strained relationships, distant friendships, or even family members who feel neglected.

This chapter is about refocusing on what truly matters. Strong relationships are a form of wealth that doesn't show up on a balance sheet, but they are just as valuable—if not more so—than financial assets.

Key Topics:

1. The Danger of Sacrificing Relationships for Wealth and Status

It's not uncommon for people to neglect their relationships when they become hyper-focused on career success. After all, society tends to reward hard work and financial achievement. But often, the unspoken cost is the weakening of personal connections.

Whether it's skipping family dinners to work late, missing important milestones in your loved ones' lives, or allowing stress from work to affect your interactions with others, the pursuit of wealth can unintentionally push people away. While it's easy to think, *"I'll make up for it later,"* many come to regret the time lost with their loved ones.

Case Study: Consider the story of Jane, a high-powered executive who spent decades climbing the corporate ladder. She was financially successful, but her relationships suffered. As her career advanced, she became increasingly isolated from her friends, her marriage ended, and her children felt distant. It wasn't until she reached retirement that she realized she had no one to share her success with. Jane had focused so much on achieving financial security that she had neglected the security of her relationships.

2. Redefining Wealth by Nurturing Personal Connections

On the other hand, there are stories of people who, despite not being extraordinarily wealthy in financial terms, live richly because they invested in their relationships. They find joy, fulfillment, and security in the bonds they've created with others, whether it's with a partner, close friends, or a supportive community. These individuals understand that true wealth is built on love, trust, and connection, not just on financial assets.

Example: Take the story of Sam, who left a high-paying corporate job to spend more time with his family and nurture his friendships. While his income took a hit, he found that his happiness and sense of fulfillment soared. Sam felt richer than ever, not because of what was in his bank account, but because of the deep relationships he had prioritized. His children felt closer to him, his marriage grew stronger, and his friendships became more meaningful. In this way, Sam redefined wealth in terms of human connection, not dollars.

3. Research on the Power of Relationships for a Happy Life

There is substantial evidence to support the idea that relationships—not wealth—are the primary drivers of happiness and well-being. Research shows that people who maintain close, supportive relationships live longer, healthier lives. The famous **Harvard Study of Adult Development**, which tracked individuals over 75 years, found that the quality of relationships was the greatest predictor of long-term happiness and well-being. The findings revealed that people with strong social connections were not only happier but also physically healthier as they aged, compared to those who were more isolated.

This research reminds us that money and material success can't replace the fulfillment we get from our relationships. While financial security is important, it is the strength of our bonds with others that ultimately leads to a meaningful, satisfying life.

Practical Takeaway:

So, how do we ensure that we are as rich in relationships as we aim to be in finances? The answer lies in making **intentional time** for meaningful connections. Here are some practical steps you can take:

1. Evaluate Your Relationships:

Take a moment to assess the current state of your relationships. Are you giving your loved ones enough time and attention? Are there relationships that you've neglected in favor of your career or financial goals? Consider where you might be falling short, and commit to reconnecting with those who matter most to you.

- **Action Step:** Make a list of the five most important relationships in your life. Write down how often you spend time nurturing these connections, and make a commitment to increase your efforts, whether through regular phone calls, family dinners, or quality time spent together.

2. Balance Career Ambitions with Relationship-Building:

It's important to strike a balance between pursuing financial success and nurturing your relationships. This might mean setting boundaries at work, carving out time for loved ones, or making career choices that align with your personal values and relationships.

- **Action Step:** Schedule regular "relationship time" into your calendar, just as you would with business meetings or work deadlines. Block off time for family outings, date nights, or simply catching up with friends over coffee.

3. Communicate Openly with Loved Ones:

If your work or financial goals have been getting in the way of your relationships, have an open conversation with your loved ones. Express your desire to make changes and show your commitment to improving your connections.

- **Action Step:** If you've been neglecting a relationship, reach out and reconnect. Be honest about your struggles to balance work and relationships, and let the person know that you want to prioritize them moving forward.

4. Create Traditions and Rituals:

One way to ensure that your relationships remain strong is to create rituals and traditions that bring people together. Whether it's a weekly family dinner, an annual trip with friends, or a monthly date night, these traditions can help maintain connection even when life gets busy.

- **Action Step:** Choose one meaningful tradition or ritual that you can start with your loved ones. Whether it's small or big, this act of togetherness can keep your relationships thriving.

Conclusion: Wealth Without Relationships is Empty

At the end of the day, the people we love are what make life truly rich. No amount of money can replace the joy of a shared laugh, the comfort of a loved one's embrace, or the peace of knowing you have a support system to rely on. True wealth is found in relationships that lift you up, support you, and bring meaning to your life. As you work toward financial success, never forget that the most valuable currency is connection.

In the grand balance sheet of life, relationships are priceless. Make sure you're investing in them as much as you invest in your financial future.

"Wealth Wisdom: Beyond the Balance Sheet"

Conclusion: Wealth Wisdom—Mastering the Mindset for Long-Term Success

As we reach the end of this journey together, let's take a moment to reflect on everything we've explored and learned. Throughout this book, we've dug deep into what it truly means to be wealthy—not just in terms of money, but in the broader, more meaningful sense of the word.

We started by questioning the typical view of wealth as purely financial and discovered that, in reality, the richest lives are built on a foundation of **mindset, discipline, emotional intelligence**, and **balance**. These qualities are the pillars that support long-term financial success, but they also help us lead lives filled with health, happiness, and meaningful relationships.

Summary of Key Lessons:

Let's recap the key lessons from our exploration of wealth wisdom:

1. Wealth is More Than Numbers:

We explored how true wealth goes far beyond the balance sheet. Yes, money is important—it gives us security, comfort, and options. But true wealth encompasses our health, relationships, sense of purpose, and emotional well-being. Money is a tool, not the end goal.

2. Patience is a Superpower:

One of the most critical lessons we've learned is that building wealth requires patience and discipline. The ability to delay gratification and let your investments—whether financial or personal—grow over time is a powerful strategy for long-term success.

3. Emotional Intelligence is Key to Financial Success:

We've discussed how emotions often drive our financial decisions more than logic. Greed, fear, anxiety, and overconfidence can lead to poor choices. The most successful people are those who have learned to manage their emotions, stay calm under pressure, and make decisions from a place of emotional intelligence rather than impulse.

4. Discipline and Habits Build Wealth:

Small, consistent actions—whether it's saving regularly, investing wisely, or making smart spending choices—are what lead to long-term financial growth. Wealth isn't built overnight; it's a slow and steady process that requires commitment and discipline.

5. Overcoming Instant Gratification:

In a world that promotes quick wins and instant rewards, learning to resist the pull of immediate gratification is essential. We've explored how true wealth is built when you focus on long-term success instead of short-term pleasures.

6. Relationships Are the Real Riches:

Wealth means little if you don't have strong, meaningful relationships. Investing in your personal connections—whether with family, friends, or your community—is as important as investing in financial assets. Love, trust, and connection are currencies that make life truly rich.

7. Health is the Greatest Wealth:

All the money in the world means little if you don't have your health. We've seen how wealth without well-being can be empty and how prioritizing your physical and mental health is crucial to enjoying the fruits of your financial success.

8. Happiness Can't Be Bought:

One of the most important lessons is that happiness doesn't come from material wealth. Beyond a certain point, more money won't make you happier. True happiness comes from finding balance, living with purpose, and nurturing the relationships and passions that make life meaningful.

Call to Action:

As you move forward from here, I encourage you to apply the principles we've discussed to your own life. This book was not just about financial strategies or success formulas; it was about **mindset**—how you think about wealth, how you approach challenges, and how you define success.

Start by reflecting on your personal relationship with money. Are your financial decisions driven by fear, impatience, or emotional reactions? Or are they guided by long-term thinking, discipline, and a clear sense of purpose?

Think about your broader wealth: Are you investing enough time and energy into your relationships? Are you taking care of your health? Are you finding fulfillment in what you do, or are you caught up in chasing financial milestones without a sense of purpose?

Wealth is a tool, not a destination. It's a resource that helps you live a fulfilling life, but it should never come at the cost of the things that matter most—your happiness, health, and connections with others.

The journey to mastering wealth is a lifelong process, but the rewards are profound. By balancing your financial goals with the deeper riches of life, you can achieve not just financial success, but true, lasting fulfillment.

Remember: True wealth is about more than money. It's about living a life that feels rich—rich in relationships, rich in purpose, and rich in well-being. As you continue on your path, keep these principles close, and you'll find that success in every dimension of your life follows.

Your Next Steps:

1. **Reflect and Reassess:** Take a moment to evaluate where you are in your wealth journey—both financially and personally. What areas of your life feel rich, and where do you feel imbalanced?
2. **Make Small Changes:** Change doesn't happen overnight. Begin by making small adjustments that

align your financial life with your values. This could be anything from automating savings, setting boundaries between work and personal time, or prioritizing self-care.
3. **Cultivate Discipline:** Stay committed to your long-term financial goals, even when distractions and temptations arise. Consistency and discipline are the foundation of building wealth that lasts.
4. **Invest in What Matters Most:** Beyond money, invest in your health, relationships, personal growth, and happiness. These are the true treasures that bring joy and fulfillment to your life.

Final Thought:

The road to true wealth isn't just about mastering your money. It's about mastering yourself—your mindset, your emotions, your habits, and your priorities. The balance between financial success and life's deeper riches is where you'll find lasting fulfillment.

So go forward, embrace wealth in all its forms, and create a life that is rich in every way that matters.

Here's to your journey toward true wealth!

"Wealth Wisdom: Beyond the Balance Sheet"

www.ingramcontent.com/pod-product-compliance
Lightning Source LLC
Chambersburg PA
CBHW070353230526
45471CB00006B/2554